COOL HAUNTS

Coloring Book

Get ready for *Master Rabbit* designed **Cool Coloring Book** series with this spooky yet mysterious **COOL HAUNTS Coloring Book**!

In this horror-themed coloring book, you will find 20 different designs that best describe the horror creatures. Each **single-sided** image has an extra copy in case you have different coloring ideas on the same image. From season icon pumpkin to kid's favorite witch, from fearful tomb to cute vampire, and from oriental dragon to unconventional skeleton, this coloring book will provide you with all the spooky elements that fits in this holiday season.

No matter you are at which level of coloring, or even for little kids, this book will give you a lot of fun. Like Master Rabbit's COOL ANIMAL Coloring Book, each of the characters in the design is wearing a pair of cool glasses.

Enjoy this coloring book to relax yourself, and expand your creativeness playing around with different color combinations. You can have fun coloring this book or make it as a party favor to your guest, or it can even serve as trick or treat gift to kids in your neighborhood.

Any question or suggestion is welcome!
Email: brothertuzi@gmail.com
Instagram: @masterabbitu

RIP

Z
Z
Z

RIP